HOW THE
BECAM

how the first sparks became visible

Poems by Simone Atangana Bekono

TRANSLATED BY DAVID COLMER

This publication has been made possible with financial support from the Dutch Foundation for Literature.

N ederlands
letterenfonds
dutch foundation
for literature

THE EMMA PRESS

First published in the Netherlands as *hoe de eerste vonken zichtbaar waren* by Wintertuin Uitgeverij in collaboration with Lebowski Publishers in 2017.
First published in the UK in 2021 by The Emma Press Ltd.

Poems © Simone Atangana Bekono 2017
English-language translation © David Colmer 2021

ISBN 978-1-912915-55-2

A CIP catalogue record of this book
is available from the British Library.

Printed and bound in the UK
by Oxuniprint, Oxford.

The Emma Press
theemmapress.com
hello@theemmapress.com
Birmingham, UK

Supported using public funding by
**ARTS COUNCIL
ENGLAND**
LOTTERY FUNDED

CONTENTS

I. 1

II. 2

III. 5

IV. 7

V. 10

VI. 12

VII. 13

VIII. 18

IX. 22

Acknowledgements 29

About the poet 30

About the translator 30

About The Emma Press 30

friction

I.

I was born in a forest

I was born and someone trained a light on me
on the birthing cloth behind me, my silhouette appeared

My silhouette opened her mouth and said
'I exist because your body exists
Cronus devouring his children
as bloodthirsty as Goya painted him
a body become unrecognisable
greedy and chaotic
not rooted in the earth'
this was all I had to go on

I heard panting and laughter: concrete, specific sounds
my silhouette was a silhouette without specific characteristics
my silhouette was mine in an incomprehensible way
she acted on my behalf, she was only there when I looked
she existed only on the cloth

Concrete, specific sounds
I wanted to be incorporated into a system of ticks and crosses
I wanted virtual, sexual, depoliticised pleasure, inside
with my chin on the edge of the desk, on the back seat of a Tesla
removed from the menu, yes
inside

II.

Who made the young me sweat in bed
with visions from the psychiatric ward
girls who've grown obsessed with the man
and the touch of the man, and the touch of the woman
that makes them realise they want to be a man

I fear the man and want to eat him up
but I am also scared that he has eaten me up
that I was born in the man's stomach
or ribcage or in a toe
and escaping from his body
has made me lose mine
I want to eat the man up the way I eat Facebook
and installation art
and have for years now eaten up
enormous amounts of light
shining on my face

I hoped to be able to eat the man up
to protect my sisters
but I feel what's left of the man gnawing at my insides
searching for a way out through my womb
my navel, my open mouth

Every inch of my body
of my thinking brain
is split into two camps
I am a single moustache hair
fallen onto the chin after an attempt at union
and the attempt at union has failed
only my silhouette seems right
I will wash down the drain of the shower or I will crumble
I will drown or suffocate in the woollen jumper
removed to facilitate copulation
meanwhile I search for electricity pylons
to hang out my shrunken body
charge it, fuse it together
because my body is more than just one body

I require a state of being that will make me superfluous and all-powerful
I want to build a corridor that leads nowhere
and lock all of my bodies up in it
so they won't harm themselves or each other
so they will be present as a single whole
without context to confirm it
billions of cancer cells that have established themselves in my father
established themselves in my mother
billions of cancer cells that have established themselves in me
waiting for the right moment
silent in a waiting room

All my poems are quiet and still
my poems have been smeared on the side of the bed
my poems are not poems
I am a puddle of blood seeping through a carpet
that tries to turn systems into words
the systems asked, 'What can you do, now you know?'
and I was quiet, deciding to go on holiday

III.

I wrote a poem about myself
I wrote five versions of myself that were male
broken, disembodied and confused
I wrote myself into the hell of being an artist and left me there to rot
I wrote beyond myself and came up with a lot of empty words:

That the moment of ignition makes or breaks all memories
that context mustn't be added, but has to arise by itself
that I put my father's urn in the fuse box when he slapped my wrist
for my dubious breasts and strange way of carrying myself
that I only exist as a projection of the brain of a white Western male:
I borrow money from a white Western male
I buy toilet paper for a white Western male
I am the white Western male's thought experiment

I am lying drunk on a floor and he asks who I am
and I am a version of Kunta Kinte forced into a mould
I feel no bond with my given name

I lie on the floor drunk and see patterns on the ceiling
the boy on the floor next to me is a child I want to acquaint
with my darkest thoughts
to destroy him
to educate him
I am an apelike jazz musician's doll

I am Sylvana, Louwiya, an enormous bum people pay money to stare at
I can present myself in hundreds of forms

I am a cool afterthought, a drum kit, I am a religious fanatic
with yellow eyeballs and a hoarse-screamed mouth, I am a court jester:
I put on a dress, I put on a flesh-coloured dress and I am
one hundred and fifty pounds of flesh without a name
language or country of origin
a nail-chewing, collapsing, bleeding anonymous entity
without a concrete goal
all energy and no purpose
I do have a good report:
well done, well brought up

I am a virus that eats itself due to a lack of matter to feed on
I am the most flesh-coloured dress you can wear
a daring choice
and oiled on a snow-white beach
standing among those hundreds of versions of myself
I ask, 'Are we already on holiday?'
I get no reply

IV.

The choir's song sticks to the feet
of the feverishly dancing priest
the house coils around him
his legs tense
all other heads in the room are bowed

All black people identify with broken people
all black people identify with abandoned people
all black people are criminal

In Hong Kong, ignore the Mong Kok express
the two people who pull you away from the sparking rails
the tramline that swallows branches as it climbs the mountain
thin air between Chinese mountains and plane wings
the flight against the Earth's rotation

Ignore the roof of the building that whispers *come closer to the edge*, the edge that whispers *look down*, the street that beckons with a thousand wrists stuck to car bumpers, thin fingers of light curling round your ribs to pull you down, and a soft whisper:

All people don't exist
all black people identify with abandoned people
and all black people don't exist

Ignore the enormous, swollen blisters on your belly, in the back of the car, screaming with pain on your way back to Holland because being in transit, relocating your soul, is accepting that temporarily you do not exist and then the pain can't either

Slowly the body bloats and grows heavier
forget the first time you realise you can no longer walk from the sofa to the toilet, the twenty lost pounds after six months in bed, the Olympic champion figure skater who veers across your screen while you piss in a pot

Because every form of self-hatred is complex and individual
all black people do not exist
'all black people' is a combination of words that starts at your teeth and extends like stretch latex over your whole body until you are broken and gasping on the floor, stripped of every form of humanity
it is only a thin layer but
it makes me unrecognisable
unliveable, ever rounder and heavier
a bucket full of water
in the middle of a swimming pool

So forget 2005
forget the cars in Naples and the drivers' fangs
the Somali handbag salesman in Rome who appeared then disappeared again
the musician in Montpelier who seemed to smell of the village where your father was born

the woman in the supermarket who reached across your mother's chest to pinch your cheek hard

Forget the pressure of this earthly existence on your chest at four in the morning, sweating from an inexplicable terror while minutes crawl over your body like spiders
all black people is a lost art, rarely mourned
an insoluble conflict

I have to spend three hours sitting in a wheelchair
and even that is exhausting
all black people sit on benches and that is exhausting
all black people watch the Oscars in bed, black people sit in the Metro
black people make their bodies smaller with big hair and tiny phones
and that is exhausting

The city is a strain
the village is a conflict zone
the natural splendour, a reflection in my rear-view mirror
'Are we already on holiday?' I asked
why didn't you answer?
all black people have gone to the seaside on holiday
bums on the beach
and even that is exhausting

V.

A chimpanzee looks at daylight for the first time
from under her bushy eyebrows
her wrinkled fingers have solved puzzles
bent tubes
and tried to protect her baby
she walks alone on a riverbank
enjoying the grass between her toes
the wind ruffles her coat
in this unknown she feels a realness
her old surroundings lacked
I want to ask her impression of the storm surge barriers
how do you take in this new reality?
do you see structures in the fields?
a purpose in your own existence?

That was how your poem went
I read it sitting on a barstool
feeling the pressure of a sun
about to explode on my fingertips
I thought you would be the end of a fever dream
waking me up with a wet flannel
simple medicine and bright eyes

You had taken me apart and been baffled by the pieces
the sun didn't hold back

and the tingling
all that energy on the point of exploding
spread from my fingers to my arms
nestled in follicles
and sprayed from my shoulders
an unhealable wound

I read your poem that said I was afraid
that I was a guttering flame, not a raging fire
that I have only just woken from my dream but
I have been awake for a very long time
I don't want to splutter and go out, I want control and that's exhausting

On this March day I am not in love
for twenty-five years now I have gone into spring
without being in love

I read your poem and thought of your bed made of old boards
two mattresses jammed into place
and the motes of dust that had settled on your clean linen
you hadn't been home for months and then you came home with me
thinking you could lift me up with the power of your will
trying to run your fingers through my hair
and ignoring me trying to disappear in you
the lack of focus in my eyes
and my body obeying your words
not your mouth

VI.

You mustn't think anything black – don't let your brain go that way
I think of black a thousand times a day and try to draw
the word out of me

My conscience says I mustn't think about it
ignore everything that makes you doubt
I think of black a thousand times a day
the footballer from Guadeloupe loves Dutch food
he says, 'Nasi goreng, roti, pea soup'

I am a country and a country that matters, and, no
I am not on holiday
that plane keeps getting pushed back
there is no hostess to ask how long this is going to take
how much longer I have to listen to the Lotto ads
I am stuck between ground and space
dead space, an unfathomable situation
a door that leads nowhere but still opens, non-stop

VII.

I was going hunting and I bought appropriate boots and a warm coat
and I didn't take a tent with me but a tarpaulin I carried in a roll on
   my back
and I walked in the bear's footsteps through the rain

The forest was aware of my scent
and my body was aware of the forest
and the birds decided to show some respect and keep their beaks shut
and the bear was preoccupied with the fish in the river and washing
the blood and shit and moss off its paws

The deer bounding ahead of me did not feel threatened
but rubbed her coat against the tree bark so I could stay close
and the trees let just enough sunlight through
and the sun was just warm enough to start water dripping
from the icy branches to mask the creaking of the tarpaulin on my back

Towards nightfall
squinting
I saw light shining on the deer's snout
and the deer standing still as if to enjoy the last bit of sunlight
I was quivering with weariness and my gun was quivering
and it seemed as if, between this moment
and the moment yet to come

In the distance between us, just a hundred feet
the grains of sand being thrown up, the drops of ice water dripping
the clouds of breath being exhaled as slowly as possible and the bear
busy with the fish in the river not much further along
the deer that might not have been enjoying the sunlight
but seemed to be waiting
I remembered the bathwater that smelt of eucalyptus
the man who walked into a lake
and said he was both here and nowhere

I saw it splitting: the distance between me and the deer
the ice water falling and the grains of sand being thrown up
the deer standing in the stripes of reddish-orange sunlight
the tarpaulin on my back not creaking and me
breathing so it was barely audible
and there was so much silence
my bones locked into place one after the other
relaxing my muscles
I saw the choices and the consequences
the enormity of the point where
the splitting began, where one became two, the deer and I
united by the as yet unmade choice
I saw my father running to school in his flip-flops
I saw my mother cutting off her braids in her bedroom
running miles to school
I saw the blisters on my little sister's hands
the stripes on my sister's back

I saw the sun reflecting on my forehead as a child
running miles to school

My bones were locked in place
and in the most insignificant part of the second there was
no breathing, no living, no pointing

Swimming in a roped off section of the Scheldt
between long strips of froth
under a sun-concealing cloud, I stopped and floated on
I was no one and nowhere and not on time
I was not quite there

When I closed my eyes the sun wasn't there either
and the cloud wasn't there
and the seagull fell silent, the party boat too fell silent
the coastguard and the inflatable animal
and all the millions of fish swimming everywhere
and nowhere in particular fell silent
being nowhere shuts you up, it protects you from hearing
a single identifiable sound and makes you drift when you
should stand firm or would like to

There is no possibility at all of finding the way back to the coast
when you have been nowhere, or come from nowhere
I can't swim, only float
listening to everything that has fallen silent
moving water off the coast

a body surrounded by bodies
surrounded by walls of other bodies
surrounded by demarcations of what a body is
or should be, or would like to be if it had a choice
trunk, limbs, head
stuffed with organs and bones
without any purpose
without roots from which it has grown
a social anthropological experiment, excised mass
a pig hung by its hind legs in a butcher's shop
ready to be sliced open from anus to neck
no longer an animal, not yet a product:

Visitors are advised against sticking their heads in the pig's rib cage
visitors are advised against becoming attached to the pig in any
    way at all

After the hunt I put my gun down on the floor
butt on the parquet, barrel aimed at the sky
the tarp I slept in rolled up against the wall
stinking of blood and shit and moss
and the deer I was no one and nowhere with
is still standing in my imagination
head turned towards the reddish-orange sun
scent smeared on the trees
my presence concealed by the prints of the bear paws

I walked in while the forest was preoccupied with the looming
    darkness
the deer and I, we made a deal in the quiet of the forest
like I made deals with the seagulls, the coastguard, the party boat
the inflatable animal and the millions of fish
in the distance between the barrel of my gun and her temple
she turned towards me, both invitation and challenge
with all the billions of things happening in the space between us
that make us merge together
announcing the moment of ignition
before the first sparks
become visible

VIII.

Burundi-Kamerundi, Yemoja and Sufi
I wrap your baby in silk!
sweet mother, I swaddle the baby in silk
until the baby itself is made of silk
a wad of wound silk
that breathes slowly and with difficulty
but it does breathe, it does
and one day it will be sure to move
no need to worry about that:
leave it behind at a bus station

And lying together in a muddy wash
smearing the mud out over our bodies
and lying together in the sun until our bodies
(and the mud!)
grow hard and crumble away when we stand
and, standing, we no longer have bodies
and need to hide like crabs without shells
between the barnacled posts crusted grey
and blue and green with coral and singing mussels

No, don't hide!
unbodied we walk from the dune to the dirt track
and from the dirt track to the road and the village square
and on the village square they follow us with their eyes
and we just laugh
then I lost the thread

There was going to be a quest, or at least a certain scenario
a poem that by detour would prove
that I can no longer own my body unless my body owns me
something like that
an appeal was going to go out and a long piece:

'Vital body, you may give up hope
if you wish, you may burn
if you wish, you may feel worn and battered
or even incorrectly assembled'

It was going to be an appeal to all bodies:
'you may think of your sorrow at every
empty chair you see at every dining table
you may think of your sorrow at every
moustache hair neatly clipped by your father
you may think of your own sorrow at every
protagonist having to carry on without love
or the lace detail on your mother's blouse
or the frozen peas you weren't allowed
to mash at home

'You may give up hope
seeing danger in every puddle
seeing every stair as the last'

Yes, give up hope, but laugh
long for an unjudged body, but laugh!
vital girl's body, laugh!
vital boy's body, laugh, child of Cronus, muddy wash
Burundi-Kamerundi
geisha with her hair up
and blackened teeth, laugh!
But gunned-down student, laugh harder
leopard hacked in two, laugh harder
man in sauna, laugh harder

When the wind is blowing hard the plant hugs
its leaves to its skeleton
like pores closing in wintry air
the dog barks louder too
on the chain in the deserted yard
and the children grow up in the bushes behind the bus station
military patterns are copied
stuck to shirts sizes s, m, l
there is fighting without bodies making contact
on the village square music is being played

Dancing dancer, laugh!
fences erected around birthplaces
torn open lion's mouth
exhausted pond
thousands of identical tower blocks in Angola, laugh!
burning sugar, broad arrow-shaped nose
oxygen mask, authentic shard vase
lost guilt, laugh!

My shell-less little crab
all bodies are symptoms of thought
all bodies do beautiful and painful things
but do not feel beautiful and painful
all bodies are greased with thick creams
wrapped in silk and
echoing laughter

IX.

You do not see clearly the evil in yourself, else you would hate yourself with all your soul. Like the lion who sprang at his image in the water, you are only hurting yourself, O foolish man. When you reach the bottom of the well of your own nature, then you will know that the vileness was from yourself.

'XXXIX: The Evil in Ourselves', Jalalu'l-Din Rumi, translated from the Persian by Reynold Alleyne Nicholson

Children with feet grey with dust

throw stones at my shadow

they think I'm ignoring them

but I'm observing the cracked earth

what's left of a dried up river

hopefully the water goddesses

got away in time

I hear gossip from the air goddesses

who tickle the leaves of the trees with their whispers

before accompanying aeroplanes to a health resort

Why am I only now writing about children and water goddesses

I used to write long letters to the women

who had patiently moulded and polished me

to the women I sat around tables with

talking about our bodies

the fluctuating degrees of bulge

we observed each other's faces with piercing looks

some call it friendship

I call it a lioness playing with her food

In *Giovanni's Room* James Baldwin says in the decisive scene
that rage made the killer lighter
fear made the victim grow heavier
rage is black water in which I am floating, in which I can drown
a treacherous sea
I have forgotten the women
I play on the beach
find bones in the sand and
all black people identify with drowned people
I said it and now I have to justify it too

So in my letter I sketch a picture of people falling into black water
a marathon is being run around black water
every now and then someone stumbles and splashes into the water
like a chicken breast on a chopping board
but then in black water
the water is black because we don't know how deep it is
someone dives, a straight line into black water
almost no ripples
someone drinks big draughts of it

There was an edge of a building
but there was also surf
the shore
the last bit of drinking water in a wrung-out landscape
the full bucket in my hand
I dig holes in the sand

to pour water into
I see myself in the black water
my reflection gulping for breath

This poem is a combination of several poems
dictated by something beautiful and painful
but I like to sleep and sometimes I get hungry
a soldier keeps getting pushed back under
every time he tries to pull himself up out of the black water
sopping-wet uniform and all
a representation of the incapacity to evade violence or death
I write down as much as I can
in the available time

I anger the water goddesses and I anger the lions
unable to remember why I walked out into the sun
I have to post my letter in the heat of the day
I have to ignore the tingling in my fingertips
my creaking collarbones
I can't remember why

People sit chained by the ankles to other people
while those people try not to fall in the water but still fall
dragging behind them the whole chain of people who absolutely
did not need to fall into the black water
nature is a causal connection
if everything is causally connected hierarchy falls away

and the deer and I are friends
it is only a coincidence that I am a hunter
and the water just happens to be black

In their panic to keep out of the water
people push other people
into the water that swallows up everyone and everything
like a monster with forty insatiable stomachs

I paddle in black water and feel my shadow panicking
trying to break free from my legs and backbone
she screams and curses me
she can't disappear in the earth's furrows
she has to go with me everywhere

We run laps around the black water
we water-ski across the black water
we flap like fish on the sand
after touching the black water
our bodies get overheated, short-circuiting
blacking out, experiencing temporary amnesia
experiencing a failure of the senses, syntax error and inflammation
we throw stones and bombs and weapons of mass destruction
    into the water
hoping they will make the bodies of all disappeared people
come flying up
but only stinking chunks of coral

fermenting ooze and merged mutated body parts
come blasting up
tongue-skinned
sixteen-headed leg monsters
thousand-fingered arm creatures

I can't believe I ever leapt into a swimming pool without fear
the drops of rain falling on me from the explosions in the black water
burn me like sulphuric acid
we hate the black water so much we want to rip off
our skin where the water has touched us
we want to burn it
this costs me ink and brainpower and associative dreams

Yemoja or Circe
or some other kind of mother perhaps
can you explain this to me?
what can I do about it, who should I talk to?
we would rather push our children into the water than go into it
    ourselves
babies flying through the air like Olympic shot-puts
thrown into the black water like bags of rubbish
sometimes we save each other from the black water
with ropes and arms and garments tied together
it takes so much effort
it takes my happiness too
it takes diamonds of time and energy

The black water doesn't move
no, that is my reflection
the tree moves
the sun flickers like a young flame over the surface
even the mountain in the distance moves, bit by bit
pulling faces
the landscape growls with life while
the water just lies there
that black fucking water

A pond or a sea or a puddle, a swimming pool
that bucket in my hand
more than anything I fear the bed of the black water
and the water frightens me because it is so easy
for me to recognise myself in the reflection of the water
and I feel guilty
because I feel incomprehensibly attracted to the black water
like us standing on the edge of a cliff
a towering cliff, looking down

ACKNOWLEDGEMENTS

The epigraph to poem 'IX' is by the Persian poet and Sufi mystic Jalalu'l-Din Rumi and comes from the poem 'The Evil in Ourselves'. This poem, together with many other Rumi poems, was translated from the Persian into English by Reynold Alleyne Nicholson and later included in the book *Selected Poems of Rumi* (2001), compiled by Paul Negri and Susan L. Rattiner. The translation of this poem is accompanied by the following note:

> *In Rumi's version of this Indian fable, the carnal self (nafs) is represented as the lion who was lured by a hare to the mouth of a deep well, where, mistaking his own reflexion for a hated rival, he sprang in and perished miserably. For the doctrine that all so-called evil is an illusion arising from the Diversity of Divine Attributes – Beauty and Majesty, Mercy and Wrath, etc. – reflected in human nature, and that only our egoism prevents us from seeing the 'soul of goodness' everywhere (...) So far as evil exists in us, its source is the unreal 'self' (nafs) by which we are separated from God. Purge the heart of 'self', and evil disappears.*

Yemoja, addressed in poems 'VIII' and 'IX', is the mother of all orishas. Orishas are deities found in the legends, including those of the Yoruba religion, practised in parts of West Africa and transported from there with slaves to America. Besides being the mother of the orishas, Yemoja is also the goddess of oceans and rivers, fertility and motherhood.

I would like to thank: David Colmer for a fantastic translation, Kim van Kaam, Anne Bosveld for her late-night cheering on, Shana and Valerie Atangana Bekono and, of course, Ina den Hollander.

ABOUT THE POET

Simone Atangana Bekono was born in 1991 and studied at Creative Writing ArtEZ, graduating in 2016 with *hoe de eerste vonken zichtbaar waren*, a collection of poems and letters which includes the poems featured in *how the first sparks became visible*. This book was republished in a commercial edition by Wintertuin Uitgeverij in collaboration with Lebowski Publishers and went on to win the Poëziedebuutprijs Aan Zee, a prize for the best Dutch-language poetry debut. In the same year, Atangana Bekono also won the prestigious Charlotte Köhler Stipendium for new Dutch writers. Her first novel, *Confrontatie*, was published in Autumn 2020 by Lebowski Publishers.

ABOUT THE TRANSLATOR

David Colmer is an Australian translator, writer and editor who lives in Amsterdam. He translates Dutch-language literature across a range of genres and has won several international prizes for his work. Recent translations include collections of the poetry of Menno Wigman and Charlotte Van den Broeck, and the classic novella *An Untouched House* by Willem Frederik Hermans. For The Emma Press he translated *Super Guppy*, a collection of poetry for children by Edward van de Vendel.

ABOUT THE EMMA PRESS

The Emma Press is an independent publisher dedicated to producing beautiful, thought-provoking books, based in Birmingham, UK. In 2020 The Emma Press was awarded funding from Arts Council England as part of the Elevate programme.